CASCADIA SCORECARD 2005

CASCADIA SCORECARD

SEVEN KEY TRENDS SHAPING THE NORTHWEST

FOCUS ON ENERGY

NORTHWESTENVIRONMENTWATCH

SEATTLE

NORTHWEST ENVIRONMENT WATCH is a not-for-profit research and communication center in Seattle, Washington. Its mission is to promote a sustainable economy and way of life throughout the Pacific Northwest—the biological region stretching from southeast Alaska to northern California and from the Pacific Ocean to the crest of the Rockies.

Library of Congress Control Number: 2004117798
ISBN 1-886093-15-6

Cover illustration, cover, and interior illustration: Jennifer Shontz
Interior design: Jennifer Shontz
Editing: Julie Van Pelt
Proofreading: Sherri Schultz

Printed by Transcontinental Printing, Canada, with vegetable-based ink on recycled paper. Text: 100 percent postconsumer waste, bleached without chlorine; map pages: 10 percent postconsumer, bleached without chlorine.

Northwest Environment Watch is a 501(c)(3) tax-exempt organization. To order publications, become a member, or learn more, please contact:
Northwest Environment Watch
1402 Third Avenue, Suite 500
Seattle, WA 98101-2130 USA
(206) 447-1880; fax (206) 447-2270
www.northwestwatch.org

CONTENTS

CASCADIA AND ITS SCORECARD

This book begins with place: Cascadia, the Pacific Northwest. Encompassing British Columbia, Idaho, Washington, Oregon, and adjoining parts of Alaska, Montana, and California (see map inside front cover), Cascadia is a region with a dawning sense of itself. Its population is larger than that of the Netherlands, its economy is larger than Russia's, and its land area is larger than France, Germany, and the United Kingdom combined—with Belgium, Italy, and Switzerland thrown in for good measure.

Named for the Cascade Mountains, for the earthquake-prone Cascadia subduction zone offshore under the Pacific, and—above all—for the cascading waterfalls that pepper the region, Cascadia has a common indigenous cultural heritage and a common history. It is bound by salmon and rivers, snowcapped mountains and towering forests. Its people share not only geography but also an aspiration: to live well in their place.

Cascadia has traditions of innovation in the public and private sectors, a well-educated populace, and a long-standing commitment to conservation and quality of life. These traits show: the Northwest retains a larger share of its natural heritage intact than perhaps any other part of the industrial world and has helped set the conservation agenda for the continent.

Still, Cascadians are in only the early phases of rising to the next great challenge for humanity: gradually but fundamentally realigning the human enterprise so that the economy and its supporting ecosystems both can thrive. Daunting, complex, systemic, seemingly quixotic, this goal—balancing people and place—is nonetheless more attainable here than anywhere else on this continent. If northwesterners can reconcile themselves with their landscapes, they can set an example for the world.

The Cascadia Scorecard measures long-term progress in the Pacific Northwest. An index of seven trends shaping the future of the region, it is a simple but surprisingly far-reaching gauge. The Scorecard's indicators—health, economy, population, energy, sprawl, forests, and pollution—provide status reports for Cascadia and, by highlighting successful communities, offer a practical vision for a better Northwest.

The Scorecard puts a spotlight on the long view and the questions that most matter over great spans of time

Above all, the Scorecard puts a spotlight on the long view and the questions that most matter over great spans of time: Are we living longer, healthier lives? Are we building strong human communities? Are we handing down to our children a place whose natural heritage is regenerating?

This 2005 edition of the Cascadia Scorecard comes a year after the original 2004 edition. That book presents a complete exposition of the seven trends: why they matter, what they mean, and what Cascadians can do about them. *Cascadia Scorecard 2005* does not replace or restate that volume; instead, it is an update and companion. It presents additional and—in all but two cases—more-current data for the seven trends, with an in-depth special section on one: energy.

Cascadians who wish to learn more about the Scorecard and how to turn its indicators in the right direction can find ample additional information—including supplementary state-, provincial-, and local-level Scorecard data and a version of this book with complete sources and citations—at *www.cascadiascorecard.org*. While there, they can sign up for free electronic updates on the Scorecard in the concise *Cascadia Scorecard News*.

Where are the citations?

A footnoted and annotated online version of *Cascadia Scorecard 2005* is posted at *www.cascadiascorecard.org*. It contains hypertext notes with full documentation in support of factual statements in this book, along with animated, time-lapse versions of many Scorecard maps. It also offers supplementary data, technical material, links, and notes on methods and definitions.

INTRODUCTION:
SECURITY SCORECARD

If news headlines are the first draft of history, then the history of 2004 in Cascadia was dominated by security and energy: fears and controversies about global terrorism and how to counter it; deployment of troops from Cascadia to war in oil-rich Iraq; and debate about that war during the most divisive American election in decades. In 2004, an oil spill of mysterious origin struck Puget Sound and, for the first time ever, gasoline prices breached $2 a gallon and briefly kissed Can $1 a liter in parts of British Columbia. The price of Alaskan crude shot above $50 a barrel and, for the first time in years, the price of petroleum regularly returned to the front pages. The conjunction of the themes of energy and security—energy security—even became a small part of the public discourse, at least in the American parts of Cascadia, with the slogan "energy independence" bandied about by politicians on both the left and the right.

Cascadia Scorecard 2005 pays close attention to security (as an organizing theme), energy (as a focal point), and their conjunction (in a special section), not in order to follow the headlines but rather to provide context for them. Cascadians' discussions of security often seem underinformed about its true nature and roots; worse, many northwesterners, including the region's leaders, seem woefully uninformed about the profound vulnerability of the region's energy system. The Cascadia Scorecard itself dictates a focus on energy: as the 2004 edition made clear, the region performs far worse on energy than on any other indicator. Finally, the region's weakness in energy actually creates staggering opportunities: a clean-energy revolution that is already gathering force promises to enhance the region's economy, quality of life, and natural heritage, even while tightening its security.

Security is not just defense against military or terrorist attacks. It is the protection of our families, communities, and homeland from profound threats, whether to our life and liberty, to our health and quality of life, or to the cultural and natural inheritance that we hold in trust for our children. It is, at root, not so much a department of government ("homeland security") or a branch of industry ("home security") as a characteristic of systems—social, economic, and physical—that makes them low-risk, resilient, and stable. "Secure" is from the Latin words *se cura*, meaning "free from care." It means reliable, safe, hard to destroy, unlikely to fail, and free from danger or fear. In practical terms, security is the control of risks to our lives and futures.

What makes Cascadians secure is not only the firepower held by their governments but also the systems that keep their prospects bright

What makes Cascadians secure, therefore, is not only the firepower held by their governments but also, and more importantly, the systems—both tangible and intangible—that keep their prospects bright. These include, at the highest level, things such as the rule of law; democratic governance; the social "capital" of civic, educational, and religious organizations; and social norms such as reciprocity and tolerance. At a less abstract level, they also include the physical form of the region's built environment and the public and private policies (from tax codes to government budgets, from land-use plans to insurance rules) that shape northwesterners' health, livelihoods, communities, and landscape.

In this full sense, security—and the systems designs that promote or degrade it—is a theme stitched through all seven Scorecard trends (see Table 1 on page 4). Cascadians' health continues to improve slowly, but enhancing economic opportunities and access to medical care (both are forms of security) would hasten progress. The economy has performed poorly of late, generating troubling insecurity for many. This economic insecurity may have contributed to a slight increase in average family size (the Scorecard's population indicator), which is often a sign of worsening living conditions for women. Energy security also seems to have declined in 2004 as northwesterners somewhat increased their consumption of expensive fuels that require safeguarding at home and overseas. And the energy system itself is profoundly insecure, even in the narrow, military sense, as detailed in the special section that begins on page 29.

Sprawl trends also have important security implications. Sprawl—a dysfunctional community design—limits transportation options, necessitating reliance on private vehicles that are dependent on vulnerable, imported fuels and crowded road space; sprawl also degrades health, worsens the air, and undermines watersheds. The sprawl indicator, while impossible to update since *Cascadia Scorecard 2004*, has mostly showed slow improvement from a disappointing record. Sprawl is Cascadia's second-worst-performing indicator.

Forest clearing, an indicator of broader trends in the status of Cascadia's natural heritage, poses a long-term risk to ecosystems that animate the region's cultures and on which northwesterners depend for flood control, water storage, biological diversity, and climate moderation. Indeed, ecosystems are models of systems that are secure in their very design: they are rich with options; they are—notwithstanding popular notions of nature's fragility—tough and resilient; and they generate the means of their own success, converting daylight and inanimate minerals into elaborate communities of life. Safeguarding ecosystems ensures northwesterners a habitable and vibrant home. Forest clearcutting slowed dramatically in the 1990s in the limited areas covered so far by the Scorecard. It has sped up again in recent years, although no data are yet available that are more current than what appears in *Cascadia Scorecard 2004*.

Finally, the Scorecard's pollution indicator shows that northwesterners hold in their bodies—and in the mother's breastmilk that feeds their newborns—toxic flame retardants called PBDEs, at 20 to 40 times the levels found in Japan and Europe. These levels are likely rising. How secure are Cascadians when hazardous compounds intervene in the gestation

Key trend	Indicator	Target: Place with world's (region's) best record	Target
Health	Life expectancy at birth, in years	Japan, 2001	81.3 years
Economy	Composite index of unemployment rate, median income, and poverty rate, 1990 = 100	Selected high-performing states, provinces, and European nations, recent years	108.6 points
Population	Total fertility rate, in children born per woman	Netherlands and Sweden, 2001–02	1.7 births
Energy	Per capita use of highway fuel and nonindustrial electricity, in gallons of gasoline-equivalent per week	Germany, 2001	7.4 gallons
Sprawl	Percentage of metropolitan-area residents in compact, transit-friendly neighborhoods	Interim target: Vancouver, BC, 2001 (European and wealthy Asian cities do better, but data not comparable.)	62 percent
Forests	Annual percentage of forests clearcut in five Cascadia study areas	Interim target: five Cascadia study areas, 1996–99 (Some forests elsewhere do better, but data lacking.)	0.4 percent
Pollution	Median concentration of toxic chemicals in breastmilk, in parts per billion (PBDEs reported here; additional chemicals forthcoming, 2005)	Japan, 2000	1.3 parts per billion

Average:

Table 1. Cascadia Scorecard 2005: The Northwest lags, on average, 32 years behind the world's leaders.

Cascadia Scorecard 2005	Scorecard gap With steady progress, how many years to match target?	Status and trend
79.2 years	13 years	Eighth best in world; improving slowly.
99.7 points	19 years	Strong by international standards; underperforming national averages since 1990; declined 1999–2003.
1.81 births	11 years	Close to world's best, but variable; improved since 2000, but worsened in 2004.
14.6 gallons	88 years	Performance very poor; improved since 2000, but worsened in 2004.
32 percent	58 years (Data problems make this figure optimistic.)	Region lags far behind Vancouver, BC; has seen slow, steady improvements since 1990.
0.5 percent	3 years (Data problems make figure optimistic.)	Stewardship improved since 1990, but worsened since 2000.
50 parts per billion	? years (Time-series data are unavailable.)	PBDEs among highest in world; concentrations likely rising; other toxics may be declining.
	32 years	Improved in 1990s, stagnant since 2000.

and nursing of the young—when the biology of motherhood itself is contaminated? A secure Cascadia would be free from such dangers.

Overall, the Cascadia Scorecard—which is designed as a gauge of long-term progress but also reflects the closely related concept of true security—shows that the Pacific Northwest has stalled in the new millennium. After making major gains in the 1990s, it has returned to the doldrums characteristic of the 1980s (see Figure 1). From 2001 to 2003, the region's aggregate Cascadia Scorecard score did not budge. On average among the six indicators for which time-series data are available (which excludes pollution), Cascadia lags 32 years behind the world's best performers on those indicators—Japan for health, Germany for energy, and so on. It would take 32 years of slow and steady progress, on average, to bring Cascadia up to what those places had already achieved by 2001 or 2002. Preliminary data suggest that 2004 may have been a fourth consecutive year of stagnation on the Scorecard. And meanwhile, the regions in the world that perform best on these indicators are not standing still but are racking up further improvements.

Figure 1. Overall, the Cascadia Scorecard's indicators made steady progress during the 1990s, but stalled in the new millennium.

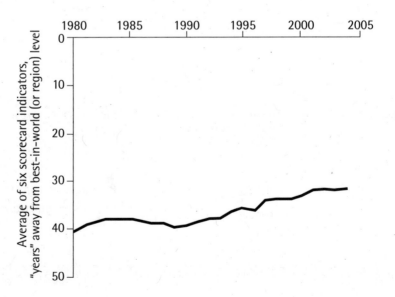

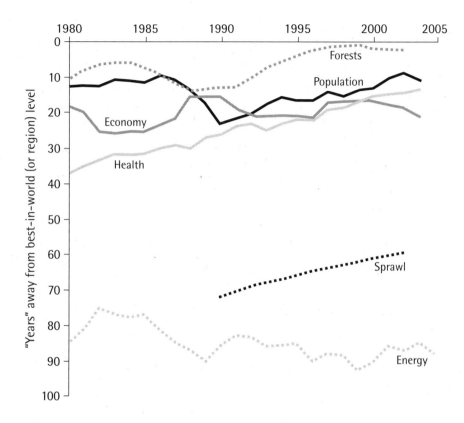

Figure 2. Cascadia scores worst on energy and sprawl.

The seven Scorecard trends have never moved in lockstep. In 2003, for example, health improved as measured by the Scorecard's indicator—lifespans—and Cascadians used energy a little more efficiently than in 2002. But those advances were counterbalanced by deterioration in economic security and an increase in family size (see Figure 2). Partial results for 2004 show that falling unemployment rates may have improved economic security but that energy efficiency worsened.

Three notes of caution are in order: First, any aggregation of such disparate trends can never be definitive; it can only be indicative, as detailed in *Cascadia Scorecard 2004*. Second, the sprawl and forest indicators remain less robust than the others. The forest indicator in particular covers only a small share of Cascadia and is, for technical reasons, less well tethered to international best practices than the other indicators. It likely gives too rosy a picture of forest stewardship.

Third, detailed time-series trends for the Scorecard's pollution indicator are not yet available and therefore are not included in Figures 1 and 2. PBDE pollution in the Northwest has grown alarmingly over the past several decades. Levels of the compounds in northwesterners' bodies appear to be at least 20 times higher today than in the mid-1980s. However, data from sediment samples, fish and wildlife, and human tissues suggest that levels of other persistent toxics targeted for elimination internationally, such as DDT, dioxins, and PCBs, are gradually falling. The net effect of these divergent trends may well be that the overall burden of persistent toxics carried in northwesterners' bodies is diminishing.

In all these cases, the key to better performance is in innovation

In all these cases, the key to better performance—the key to greater security—is in innovation: new technologies, business models, and public policies that can better align Cascadia's economy and way of life with its shared aspirations. Such systemic innovations are already emerging. (Some of the most promising are detailed in the concluding chapter, "Security by Design.") Indeed, they have been gathering momentum for some time, proving their potential and, often, their profitability. All that is lacking is a critical mass of northwesterners acting in their own lives and through the region's governments, businesses, and civic organizations to speed the change.

1. HEALTH

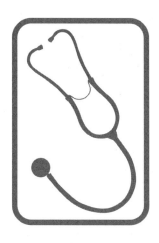

Northwesterners' health, arguably the most fundamental form of security, continues to improve, slowly but steadily. A baby born in 2002, the most recent year for which data are available across the entire region, could expect to live past 79 years of age—about a month longer than a baby born in 2001. This gradual increase in longevity continues a trend: life expectancies in Cascadia have grown by nearly four years since 1979 (see Figure 3).

Life expectancy is the best single measure of a population's health. Lifespan reflects all of the diseases, accidents, and lifestyle choices that shorten people's lives, as well as the effectiveness of medical care. Contrary to first impressions, it does not simply reflect medical practices that extend lives without improving them: across nations, every added month of life expectancy tends to bring more than a month of good health.

Health trends are not uniform across the region, as the life-expectancy map on page 40 makes clear. The 49th parallel, which marks the boundary between British Columbia and the Northwest states, also delineates a profound divide in human health. Residents of British Columbia can expect more than 2 additional years of life, compared with their counterparts in Washington, Oregon, and Idaho. Life expectancy in the province was 80.5 years in 2002, versus about 78.4 in the Northwest states. In fact, British Columbia is the healthiest Canadian province, and Vancouver is Canada's healthiest big city. A Vancouver resident can expect 81.1 years of life, nearly on a par with the life expectancy of Japan, which has the longest life expectancy of any nation in the world.

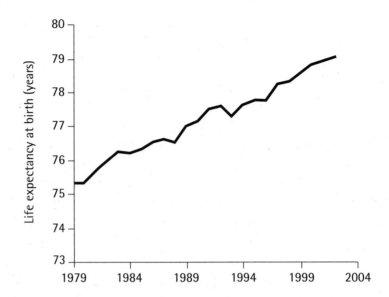

*Figure 3. Average life
expectancy in Cascadia
has increased by nearly
four years since 1979.*

The international boundary is just one of many lines, both political and social, that demarcate health outcomes in the Northwest. Within each state or province of Cascadia, there are divides in the quality of health that are just as deep as the one that separates British Columbia from the American Northwest.

No place shows such health discrepancies more clearly than greater Portland. Residents of Washington County, the largely suburban county to the west of the city, home to Nike and Intel, can expect to live about 79.7 years. But for residents of adjacent Multnomah County, which contains the city of Portland proper, life expectancy is 3 years shorter.

It might be tempting to attribute the difference in life expectancy between the two counties to the stresses and risks of urban living. But that explanation is wrong. All else being equal, living in a sprawling suburban community—where low densities discourage walking and biking—is a drag on health. In highly sprawling US cities, for example, nearly one in ten adults, on average, has a chronic health problem that can be traced to low-density, car-dependent community design.

The far likelier explanation for the difference in health between Multnomah and Washington counties concerns economic security and, specifically, income disparities: Multnomah County has pockets of poverty that are both larger and deeper than those found in Washington County. And poverty worsens health, not only because the impoverished have less access to high-quality medical care, but also because they tend to be under greater stress and to have fewer of the close social ties (call it "community security") that can help buoy health. Studies from around the world show that economic inequality and social isolation are major barriers to health.

Similar divides are seen in the state of Washington: life expectancy in relatively wealthy King County is about two years longer than in more financially distressed Pierce and Yakima counties.

Although health is generally improving in the Northwest states, longevity gains have lagged behind other parts of the industrialized world. Indeed, the real issue might be not why BC lifespans are rising so quickly, but why the gains in Idaho, Oregon, and Washington have been so meager. The keys to matching or bettering BC's health status are likely enhanced access to medical care and, as important, innovations in economic and social policy that drive lasting reductions in poverty.

2. ECONOMY

Economic well-being is conventionally gauged by gross domestic product (GDP)—the total output of a region's economy. But in a society in which wealth is increasingly concentrated in a few hands, GDP may rise even as the fortunes of middle- and lower-income Cascadians falter.

In order to gauge the economy's real-world effects on working families, the Cascadia Scorecard tracks a fourfold index that integrates typical household incomes, the unemployment rate, the poverty rate, and the child poverty rate. Economic security is also important to measure because the fortunes of ordinary people are so closely tied to the region's future. For Cascadia, one of history's richest places, economic insecurity is a systemic flaw, one that slows long-term progress and generates unnecessary risks. For example, poverty slows learning in children (ultimately making the workforce less competitive), amplifies crime and delinquency (eroding quality of life), and increases the prevalence of teen pregnancy (weakening families).

The year 2003—the last year for which complete income and poverty data for US states are available—was a disappointment, the culmination of four consecutive years of declining economic security in the region. By the end of the year, virtually all of the economic gains that accrued to middle- and lower-income families during the late 1990s had evaporated (see Figure 4). Partial data for 2004—falling unemployment rates for the first ten months of the year—suggest that the Northwest states may be shaking themselves from their economic doldrums. But they have a lot of ground to make up.

In 2003, for example, poverty rates in the Northwest states stood at their highest levels since 1995, elevated by a striking increase in the share of children who are impoverished. And nearly one in eight

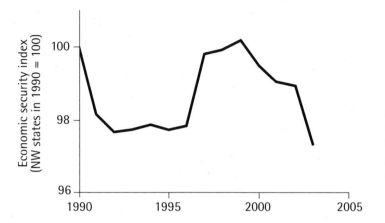

Figure 4. By 2003, the economic gains attained by the Northwest states in the late 1990s had evaporated.

residents of the Northwest states lived below the federal poverty line, meaning that more US northwesterners than ever before could be called poor: 1.3 million in total, including half a million children.

In part, poverty peaked because jobs became scarce. Oregon had the highest unemployment rate in the country in 2003, briefly topping 9 percent; it was the worst year to look for a job in the state since 1986. Washington fared only slightly better, though Idaho's unemployment rate was considerably lower than its western neighbors'. Overall, the three states added 416,000 new residents between 2000 and 2003, but only 6,300 new jobs. Many eligible workers simply gave up looking for work—which, ironically, made unemployment statistics look unduly rosy. Potential workers are considered unemployed only if they are actively looking for paid jobs. With employment so scarce, incomes stagnated: the typical household earned slightly more in 2003 than in the previous year, but nearly $4,000 less than in 1998, adjusted for inflation.

Complete poverty and income data for British Columbia were available only for 2002. But the province's economic performance was similar to its southern neighbors': poverty, child poverty, and unemployment became more prevalent in 2002, and median income declined slightly from the previous year. Still, these measures had changed little over the

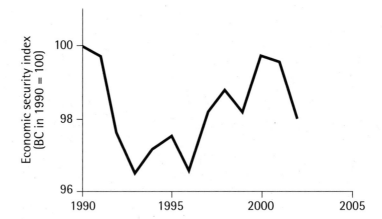

Figure 5. British Columbia's economy took a step backward in 2001 and 2002.

previous decade: unlike the rest of Canada, British Columbia appears to have made little headway in improving the economic security of the poor and the middle class (see Figure 5).

Perhaps the single most important key to improving economic security in Cascadia is a shift in public consciousness and political debate. If northwesterners replaced GDP as the Northwest's bellwether measure of livelihood with the Scorecard's economy indicator, the region would see a gradual but profound realignment in public policies. Systems currently designed to boost growth for its own sake would move instead to strengthen economic security. For one thing, this shift would move poverty reduction, which currently languishes as an objective of welfare and social-service programs, to the economic-development heart of policymaking in the region.

3. POPULATION

Cascadia's average family size improved in 2002, reaching an all-time low of 1.78 births. But it reversed course and expanded again in 2003 to 1.81 births (see Figure 6). Average family size (lifetime births per woman or, more precisely, the "total fertility rate") is an excellent gauge of women's—and families'—well-being. In nations where women have more opportunities and greater equality with men, women tend to have smaller families, later in life; in particular, they have fewer teen births and markedly lower rates of unplanned pregnancies.

Growing up in economic insecurity tends to boost women's birthrates, because young women with few options or hopes for the future often look on motherhood as one meaningful way of life they cannot be denied. Physical and sexual abuse of girls—among Cascadia's most important and most hidden forms of insecurity—also markedly raises birthrates in girls' teen years. Abuse victims often accept childbearing in hopes that their child's love will make them feel whole again.

Family size is also a gauge of the Northwest's population growth, which powerfully shapes the Northwest's environment. Births—unlike migration—account for the share of this population growth that has global as well as local implications.

As displayed in the map on page 41, average family size varies dramatically across the Northwest. British Columbians have the smallest families, at 1.4 lifetime births per woman, likely as a result of lower poverty rates and better access to reproductive health care and contraceptive services. Idaho families are the largest at 2.3 children, on average. Washington and Oregon fall in between, at 1.9. Localities differ even more dramatically. Over their lives, for example, women in Yakima County in eastern Washington have an average of 2.7 children. Near

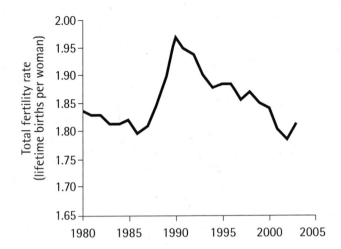

Figure 6. Cascadia's average family size reached a record low in 2002, but increased in 2003.

Boise, in suburban Canyon County, Idaho, women have 2.6 children. But women in Lane County, Oregon, which surrounds Eugene, have only 1.5 children apiece, and their counterparts in Vancouver, British Columbia, have an average of just 1 child each.

Family size tends to be inversely proportional to population density: urban counties typically have the smallest families, suburban counties have larger ones, and rural areas have the largest. To some extent, this pattern is a reflection of households with children seeking affordable single-family housing and finding it in the suburbs and beyond. But rural economic insecurity also plays a large role. Notable exceptions to the rule are rural areas such as northern Idaho and rural western Oregon, which have small families.

Declining total fertility rates, especially when they stem from falling birthrates among very young women, are a hopeful sign for societies that aspire to gender equality. The world's leading nations in women's equality and pro-family policies, such as excellent child care and paid parental leave, are the Netherlands and Sweden. They have total fertility rates of around 1.7.

Cascadia can match this rate by better preventing unplanned pregnancies. Some 9 percent of births in the Northwest states (but fewer in British Columbia) result from "unwanted" pregnancies: they are conceived accidentally at a time when the mother wants no children, or no more children. Another 30 percent come earlier in women's lives than these women intended. The prospects for life are better for children who are born wanted. Children conceived intentionally receive better prenatal care and are less likely to have dangerously low weights at birth or to die in infancy. They display superior verbal development in their early years and are less likely to endure abuse and neglect. Consequently, fewer wanted children end up in the child welfare system, including juvenile courts and foster care. Wanted children are more secure.

A worthy population goal for Cascadia would simply be that every child be born wanted.

Universalizing one-stop access to emergency contraception at pharmacies, as British Columbia and parts of Washington have already done, could be the next step toward that goal. Princeton University researcher James Trussell calculates that this step could cut the unintended pregnancy rate (and the abortion rate) by as much as half. In 2005, the US Food and Drug Administration will rule on a proposal to make the emergency contraceptive Plan B available without a prescription to everyone over the age of 16.

4. SPRAWL

Sprawl—dispersed, compartmentalized, automobile-oriented urban development—figures into the Scorecard because it contributes to a distressing array of ills. Sprawl locks northwesterners into an auto-dependent lifestyle, with an attendant burden on their pocketbooks, the world's oil fields, and the planet's atmosphere. Sprawl also consumes farmland and open space and ruins lowland ecosystems. It endangers health by putting people behind the wheel (and in danger of crashing) an average of nine hours a week, by tainting the air and water with toxic pollutants, and by turning walking into recreation rather than transportation. In short, sprawl is a paradigm case of an insecure system: a community design that endangers the community's residents and their home place.

The Scorecard measures the best single indicator of sprawl: residential density, or the number of people who live on each acre. Density reveals to what extent growing populations are consuming new land. And studies of more than 100 cities on four continents show that neighborhood density is the most important determinant of how much people drive.

Cascadia Scorecard 2004 showed that greater Vancouver, British Columbia, controlled sprawl better than any other Northwest metropolis, with nearly two-thirds of the city's residents living in compact neighborhoods (those with population densities of 12 or more people per acre). Although more recent data on the region's sprawl trends have not become available, a fresh analysis of 12 non-Cascadian cities from across the continental United States puts the Northwest cities in better context. Even among this larger pool of cities, Vancouver's sprawl record is still the cream of the crop. Of the non-Cascadian cities, the least sprawling was—perhaps surprisingly—Las Vegas, Nevada. Half of Las Vegas residents live in compact neighborhoods, twice as large a share as in greater Seattle or Portland (see Las Vegas map on page 42).

Study of these other US cities did reveal that Portland is a model of a different sort: while not as compact as Vancouver, it is a star at protecting rural land from suburban development (see Portland map on page 43). Among the non-Cascadian cities, only Sacramento and Salt Lake City did better, and only by the slimmest of margins. Apparently, Oregon's land-use laws, in place since the 1970s, have helped curtail the loss of open space at the urban fringe.

Portland's performance is even more impressive considering another pattern that emerges among non-Cascadian cities: cities in arid zones sprawl little, compared with cities where water is abundant. This dry-ness largely explains the impressive smart-growth performance of the desert city of Las Vegas. It also explains why Denver, Phoenix, Salt Lake City, and Sacramento are more compact than water-rich cities such as Portland and Seattle. In arid zones, it is costly to provide water service to dispersed suburbs; water scarcity serves as a natural brake on low-density sprawl.

Compared with other rainy US cities, Portland's sprawl record truly shines. If greater Portland had sprawled like the typical high-rainfall city over the 1990s, it would have lost at least 150 additional square miles of rural land and open space on the urban fringe—an area larger than the city of Portland itself. That area would have almost doubled if Portland had mirrored Charlotte, North Carolina, the most sprawling of the cities studied (see Charlotte map on page 42). In arid regions, the natural environment limits sprawl; in Portland, the policy environment did.

Unfortunately, Portland's policy environment changed in November 2004 with the passage of Ballot Measure 37, which made it dramatically more complicated and expensive for governments to implement land-use plans. The result: despite greater Portland's strong record in protecting farmland at the urban fringe, its future success is uncertain.

Compared with other rainy US cities, Portland's sprawl record truly shines

The challenge for Oregon cities, as for cities elsewhere in Cascadia, is to develop means to grow up, rather than out, even in the era of Measure 37. One lesson of Vancouver's success is to aggressively promote dense, walkable downtown development through planning and through public investments in parks, transit, and other urban amenities (but not in over-building the road network). Pulling growth inward helps tremendously, even when policies such as Measure 37 make it harder to discourage low-density development on the urban edge.

5. FORESTS

Monitoring the health of the Northwest's ecosystems may be the Score-card's greatest challenge, given the lack of good data on the condition of natural systems, the innate complexity of these systems, and the many stresses they endure. As a limited but informative substitute, the Score-card tracks forest cover in five areas of the region by measuring acres of clearcuts over a 30-year period with imagery from the NASA Landsat system (see map of forest study areas on page 39). Tracking clearcuts provides a rough gauge for how extensively humans have altered the forests of the Northwest—and for how effectively northwesterners are safeguarding their distinctive natural heritage. Clearcut logging alters natural ecosystems and constricts the habitat of old-forest species. All forms of logging emit greenhouse gases, which are responsible for global warming, and require road building, which causes erosion and degrades streams. Clearcuts, then, indicate the gradual undermining of the ecological security of Cascadia's human residents and the regional economy on which they depend.

Because the Landsat system suffered extended malfunctions, up-dated forest trend data from these study areas have been unavailable since *Cascadia Scorecard 2004*. That volume showed that, in all the study areas, the rate of cutting fell over time and then rebounded mod-estly in recent years.

During 2004, many signs suggested accelerated clearcutting. In September, the Washington Board of Natural Resources approved a large hike in the cut rate on the state's public holdings. Strong demand for home building in the United States fed a boom in the timber indus-try in British Columbia. The province also rewrote its logging rules to accelerate the cut on the coast. In the interior, the province has been

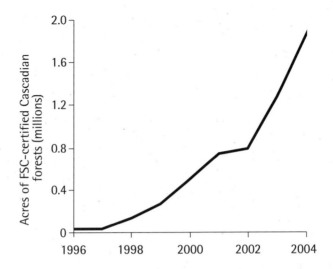

Figure 7. Since 1996, the number of acres of Cascadian forests certified by the Forest Stewardship Council has grown rapidly.

encouraging accelerated logging in pine forests in (arguably vain) hopes of heading off a massive climate change–induced infestation of mountain pine beetles. The US federal government has sought to accelerate logging on its lands, which cover a quarter of Cascadia, through the deceptively named "Healthy Forests Initiative."

A more encouraging trend in 2004 was the rapid growth in forests managed in compliance with the demanding standards of the Forest Stewardship Council (FSC; see Figure 7). Some 1.8 million acres of Cascadian forests—roughly 1 percent of Cascadia's forestland—had passed muster with FSC certifiers by December; fully 36 percent of the total was in the hands of the Potlatch Corporation in Idaho. This well-run land is a piece of the region's ecological security infrastructure.

A comparison of forest clearing on state and provincial lands inside the Scorecard's study areas provides fresh insight into how the governments of British Columbia, Oregon, and Washington manage forests that they hold in public trust. It shows that Oregon has been the most reluctant to log its state lands. Washington cut the largest share of its lands, but British Columbia—with its vast holdings—cut an order of magnitude more forest per day.

Study area	State- or provincial-owned forestland clearcut, 1971–2002	
	Cumulative share	Average acres per day
Southern Oregon	17 percent	2
Central Cascades, OR	11 percent	5
Central Cascades, WA	20 percent	10
Olympic Peninsula, WA	30 percent	15
Williams Lake region, BC	21 percent	124
Inland Rainforest, BC	21 percent	104

Table 2. Over three decades, Washington clearcut the largest share of its state lands, but British Columbia cut far more area.

In the Scorecard's southern Oregon study area, centered on Roseburg, the Oregon Department of Forestry authorized the clearcutting of 17 percent of state-owned forests from 1971 to 2002, a rate of roughly 2 acres per day (see Table 2). State lands were relatively lightly touched compared with the vastly larger private holdings in the study area, of which 35 percent were clearcut. Even the nearby national forest and Bureau of Land Management holdings in the study area were clearcut more severely; nearly 22 percent of these federal lands were cut.

Further north, in the Central Cascades study area spanning the Oregon-Washington border between Mount Hood and Mount Rainier, Oregon allowed 11 percent of state forests to be cleared. Across the Columbia River, in the larger forest holdings of the state of Washington, the rate of clearcutting was almost twice as high (see Figure 8). To the west, in the Olympic Peninsula study area, clearcutting on state lands exceeded that in the Olympic National Forest. In British Columbia's two

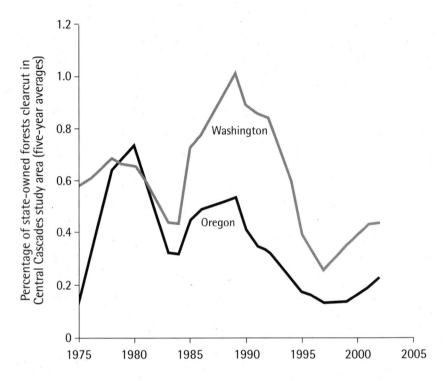

Figure 8. In the Central Cascades, Washington's state-owned forests were logged more heavily than Oregon's in the past 30 years.

large study areas, virtually all logging is on provincial land: 91 percent of the area logged was on the 85 percent of forests held by the province.

A decisive step toward institutionalizing careful management of state and provincial lands would be for governments to seek FSC certification of public forestland. Proposals to do so in Oregon and Washington made remarkable headway in 2004, but so far, the distinction of being the first Cascadian state or province to win certification as a globally responsible forest steward remains unclaimed.

6. POLLUTION

Within the body of each Cascadian is a thin broth of dozens, or even hundreds, of industrial chemicals, many of which did not exist a century ago. Some of these compounds may be harmless. Others, science has shown, are not. The most troublesome share three characteristics. They are slow to break down, persisting in the environment for years or decades after they are released. They accumulate in living things, including human bodies. And they are toxic, interfering with hormonal activity or other bodily functions, often at unimaginably small concentrations.

Such persistent, bioaccumulative toxics ought to be understood for what they are: security threats, and systemic ones at that. They endanger human health and child development, sometimes for generations, along with the health of orcas and other wildlife. They undermine industries that work in direct concert with the region's natural heritage, such as fishing and farming. They impose colossal financial burdens on both citizens and businesses for cleanup, and those burdens divert capital from productive investments in the future to the least productive ones—correcting old mistakes. The inverse of security by design, they generate harm that compounds itself over time and space.

Perhaps the most infamous persistent toxic is the pesticide DDT, which was finally banned in the 1970s. Levels of this chemical menace in northwesterners' bodies and environment have declined since, but this remedial success has not yet taught its lesson. The full class of synthetic compounds deserves treatment under the precautionary principle, an ethic of environmental management codified in international agreements and many nations' laws. The principle dictates that producers prove the safety of substances first, before they put them into widespread use.

In the late 1990s,
scientists started
noticing an
alarming rise in
environmental
concentrations of
flame retardants
known as PBDEs

Unfortunately, the Cascadia Scorecard, which analyzes human breastmilk from mothers across the Northwest for persistent toxics, shows that this principle has been largely ignored.

Take, for instance, the flame retardants known as PBDEs (polybrominated diphenyl ethers). For decades, these compounds have been added to furniture foams, industrial textiles, electronics, and other products found in homes and offices. But in the late 1990s, scientists started noticing an alarming rise in environmental concentrations of PBDEs. The findings were uniform: PBDE concentrations were increasing rapidly in the blood, fatty tissues, and breastmilk of humans, as well as in fish, wildlife, and the sediments of water bodies. In Sweden, for example, PBDE levels in human breastmilk rose roughly 60-fold between 1972 and 1997.

Closer to home, PBDE concentrations rose more than 10-fold in samples of human breastmilk from Vancouver, British Columbia, between 1992 and 2002, and up to 12-fold in whitefish from British Columbia's portion of the Columbia River system between 1992 and 2000. High PBDE levels also showed up in fish in Washington and in Puget Sound orcas. Globally, PBDE levels in the environment and in people appeared to be rising exponentially, doubling every two to five years.

While scientists were becoming aware of the remarkable rise of PBDEs in living things, other researchers were discovering that PBDEs were far more toxic than they had previously believed. Studies of laboratory animals showed that PBDEs can, among other things, impair memory and learning, alter behavior, delay sexual development, and disturb thyroid hormone levels. PBDEs are similar, both in their chemical structure and in the harm they cause, to PCBs (polychlorinated biphenyls), a now-banned class of chemicals that have been linked with a host of developmental delays and other adverse health effects in children and wildlife.

Because the lion's share of the most-toxic forms of PBDEs has been used in North America, levels on this continent are the highest on the planet. Northwest levels are no exception.

In 2004, Northwest Environment Watch completed an analysis of breastmilk samples donated by 40 Pacific Northwest mothers—10 each from Montana, Oregon, Washington, and British Columbia. Testing breastmilk has clear advantages over testing other body fluids or tissues. Monitoring human breastmilk, particularly if samples are taken soon after birth, provides a useful indicator for exposure levels in early fetal development, the period when humans are most susceptible to toxics. And unlike blood or tissue samples, breastmilk can be collected inexpensively and without invasive medical procedures. It is also high in fat, and PBDEs collect in fat, which makes it possible to run comprehensive tests with small amounts of milk. Breastmilk tests may even be a reliable proxy for measuring PBDE levels from environmental exposures in males of a similar age.

Chemical analysis of northwesterners' breastmilk revealed high levels of the flame retardants in every sample tested. Levels in Cascadia were among the highest in the world. The median level among Northwest mothers was 50 parts per billion; the maximum concentration was 321 parts per billion. In contrast, tests of blood samples from Japan and breastmilk samples from Sweden showed median concentrations of 1.2 and 2.1 parts per billion, respectively (see Figure 9).

Scientists are uncertain about the developmental effects that may be caused by such levels of PBDEs. No tests of PBDEs have been conducted on humans. But some scientists believe that levels found in the most exposed northwesterners are comparable to those that have been found to affect development in laboratory animals.

Though contaminants in breastmilk are certainly unwelcome, an extensive body of research demonstrates that breastmilk is still the best food for babies, and that breastfeeding is one of the most important contributors to infant health. Infants who are not breastfed do not receive optimal nutrition, important hormones, protective immune factors, and promoters of brain development. Among other benefits, breastfeeding reduces infant mortality and may lead later in life to lower rates of obesity and heart disease.

After the evidence of PBDEs' risks mounted, regulators finally took action. The US Environmental Protection Agency persuaded the

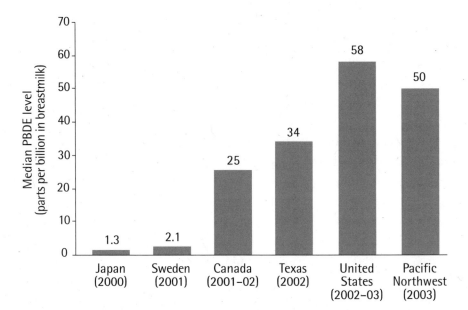

Figure 9. Levels of PBDEs in the Pacific Northwest are 20 to 40 times higher than levels in Japan and Sweden.

manufacturer of the most troubling forms of PBDEs to remove their products from the market; the manufacturer was scheduled to cease production in December 2004. California, Maine, and Hawaii passed legislation to ban or restrict some forms of the compounds. Canada is considering taking similar action. And recently, the State of Washington drafted a plan to ban most forms of PBDEs from commerce in the state and to investigate ways to remove PBDEs from people's homes.

This belated response is encouraging, but it is not proof of how well Cascadia secures itself from chemical attackers. To the contrary, it is another in a long string of tragic cases—lead, arsenic, asbestos, DDT, PCBs, dioxins, and many others—that demonstrate the region's failure to look before it leaps by observing the precautionary principle. By the time the evidence of a compound's harm is incontrovertible, it is often too late to contain the hazards. Perhaps soon, the region will embrace the systemic innovation of requiring better safety tests before a compound is used in commerce, just as the national governments of the United States and Canada already do for new medicines and food additives.

7. SPECIAL SECTION: ENERGY AND SECURITY

Of all the commodities produced and consumed in Cascadia, none casts a longer security shadow than energy. This shadow extends to the economy and the environment. It also extends to some profound but little-known physical vulnerabilities—the main focus of this chapter. In the age of what *New York Times* columnist Thomas Friedman calls "people of mass destruction," Cascadia's energy system, long among its greatest strengths, has become one of its greatest security vulnerabilities. This is true not only in the long-term sense that the energy system is slowing the economy and changing the climate, but also in the conventional, military sense: a lone terrorist could bring Cascadia's economy to its knees for days; an organized band could make it weeks or months.

The region has massive dams that generate cheap hydropower, but that power is transmitted across mountains and deserts on power lines that are impossible to defend against hikers with backpacks of explosives. The Northwest runs on oil and gas from Alaska and Alberta, but it receives those fuels through a handful of pipelines that are equally indefensible. And, unfortunately, Cascadia's energy security appears to have worsened in 2004 as per-person consumption of energy increased despite a slack economy and high fuel prices.

The only good news is that the same energy transition that can protect the region from malice—decentralizing and diversifying Cascadia's energy system—can also generate thousands of new jobs, help restore the region's natural heritage, and breathe new life into farm communities.

ENERGY ARTERIES

The region's vulnerability starts with oil, the lifeblood of Northwest transportation. Cascadia produces virtually none of its own petroleum (and hardly any of its natural gas), nor does it have appreciable reserves in the ground. Much of Cascadia's oil comes from Alaska's Prudhoe Bay, through the Trans-Alaska Pipeline, to a loading dock in Valdez, Alaska, where it is pumped onto tankers that sail to five refineries along Puget Sound. Most of the oil, once it is refined into products, reaches consumers through the Olympic Pipeline (see map of oil pipelines on page 46).

At about 20 inches in diameter, and typically buried just a few feet underground, the Olympic Pipeline connects northern Washington with Portland and Eugene along a well-marked route through forests, farm fields, and residential neighborhoods. It delivers the majority of Washington's and more than three-quarters of Oregon's gasoline. In 1999, it sprang a leak that caught fire, killing three boys along Whatcom Creek in Bellingham.

The demographic heart of British Columbia gets most of its oil from Alberta through the Trans-Mountain Pipeline, which traverses hundreds of miles of hinterlands before reaching the lower Fraser Valley and, eventually, connecting with the Olympic Pipeline. The province has just two refineries, in Prince George and Burnaby, while Idaho, Oregon, and Cascadia's parts of California and Montana have none.

These pipelines are radically exposed to mischief. The Trans-Alaska is 800 miles long, sits elevated above the ground for more than 400 of those miles, and was long ago deemed indefensible by the Pentagon. It is aging and corroding and is near the end of its design life. It has already been sabotaged once, bombed twice, and shot more than 50 times, most recently in 2001 by a drunk with a hunting rifle. In 1999, a disgruntled Canadian ex-convict was apprehended just months before he had planned to blow up three key segments in midwinter, when repair could have taken months. He had begun assembling 14 sophisticated bombs and had pinpointed the pipeline's weak points. Other near misses are much rumored but classified. The US Department of Homeland Security did reveal in 2004 that its late 2003 "elevated terror alert" was motivated by intelligence suggesting terrorists might attempt to ignite the fuel stockpiles at the pipeline's Valdez terminus. The opening of the Arctic National Wildlife Refuge to oil extraction, if it happens, would redouble and extend Cascadia's dependence on this single, insecure pipeline.

The Olympic—and two lesser pipelines that supply the inland Northwest—are, if anything, more worrisome. If the Trans-Alaska is impaired, Cascadia could still buy tankerloads from more distant sources, as Washington already does for a quarter of its crude. But losing the Olympic would create a distribution meltdown that could take weeks to rectify; Cascadia doesn't have the vehicles or loading facilities to replace the pipelines. When a similar gasoline pipeline ruptured in Arizona in 2003, it took authorities almost two weeks to *begin* repairs and 17 additional days to complete them. Average fuel prices in Phoenix rose 60 cents a gallon and did not revert to their preaccident level for four months.

In Cascadia, therefore, dependence on imports of Middle East oil is a smaller security threat than is the domestic oil infrastructure. And al Qaeda has already targeted such systems, calling oil the "umbilical cord and lifeline of the crusader community."

The region's natural gas infrastructure is the same story but in some ways worse. The Northwest's natural gas comes across the Canadian Rockies through two pipelines and from Wyoming and other Rocky Mountain states via a third (see map of natural gas pipelines on page 47). These pipelines are just as vulnerable to sabotage as the oil pipelines they sometimes parallel. The main differences are that they are more explosive and they have no substitutes. Unlike liquid fuels, natural gas cannot simply be put in a truck or railcar and wheeled to its destination. It has to be compressed or cooled first. The region does stockpile natural gas underground in two locations near Portland, to buffer against shortages, but the pipelines leading from those facilities are as vulnerable as all the others.

In Cascadia, dependence on imports of Middle East oil is a smaller security threat than is the domestic oil infrastructure

Cascadia also has four small liquefied natural gas (LNG) facilities, in Nampa, Idaho; Newport and Portland, Oregon; and Plymouth, Washington. These plants cool gas and store it at –259 degrees Fahrenheit. Larger LNG facilities were proposed in 2004 by at least three companies, two for the lower Columbia River and a third for Coos Bay on the Oregon coast—all of them intended to receive fuel from around the Pacific Rim. LNG is quite safe in most circumstances, but it does carry one special danger. Lighter than water but heavier than air, it can flow across large areas and, if conditions are exactly right as it warms and vaporizes, a spark can ignite it in a massive explosion. The LNG payload of standard marine tankers is the energy equivalent of 50 Hiroshima-size bombs, which may make tankers targets for terrorists. Fortunately, successfully igniting a spill would be difficult.

Power-transmission lines constitute a third type of energy artery in Cascadia. Three long-distance power lines connect the Northwest states' power grid with California's; a fourth connects it with British Columbia's; and a fifth with the northern plains' (see map of transmission lines on page 48). All of these lines, like the approximately two dozen major wires connecting dams and other generators with cities, are also vulnerable to attack. The power network is more secure than the pipeline infrastructure, because it has so many more routes and connections. On the other hand, it is less stable: it is a massive, interconnected balancing act. Losing three key lines or power plants is more than the system is designed to bear, and losing even two creates some probability of cascading blackouts. In the summer of 2003, the malfunction of a generating station and transmission line in Ohio unleashed a bizarre chain reaction that eventually shut down power for as much as four days in areas stretching north into Canada and east to the Atlantic seaboard. Along the way, any number of system weaknesses and operator errors worsened matters, revealing how imperfect the grid actually was.

Transmission lines are vulnerable to attacks with weapons: rifle fire knocked out transmission systems three times between December 2003 and July 2004 in Oregon and Washington alone. But they are also vulnerable to hand tools. In November 2004, an attacker loosened some bolts and let gravity fell a transmission tower in Wisconsin, interrupting electricity to the Milwaukee airport and 17,000 other utility customers. *USA Today* reported that authorities admitted, "Anyone with a common wrench could have removed the standard, two-inch bolts that connected the tower to the base." This sabotage took place just one year after Michael Devlyn Poulin of Spokane, Washington, was finally apprehended by the FBI. Over a period of weeks, Poulin, who described himself to the Associated Press as "62 years old, overweight, arthritic, diabetic, half-blind and a cancer patient," unscrewed bolts with impunity from about 20 transmission towers across the Northwest and California. Poulin's avowed purpose was not to crash the grid but to illustrate its vulnerability. He succeeded.

The oil, gas, and power distribution systems are triply insecure in combination

The oil, gas, and power distribution systems are all insecure individually, but they are triply insecure in combination. Pipelines need electricity to run their pumps and controls. Cascadia's electric grid needs fuel for the natural gas turbines that account for one-seventh of its generating capacity. And many of the region's pipelines share the same routes with each other and with power lines. The pipelines are literally underneath the wires. In at least one place in the region—prudence argues against naming it—a night's work with a backhoe could sever regionally vital arteries for oil, natural gas, *and* electricity.

Cascadia's energy system casts a shadow on security in other ways as well. Economically, the energy system's famous upside—inexpensive, nonpolluting, plentiful hydropower—has proved to have a downside too. It lured the Northwest into wasteful ways; inefficient electric space- and water-heating equipment, for example, consumes half of residential electricity in the Northwest states and more than a quarter in British Columbia. Now, with demand far outstripping hydropower supply and prices up, this installed equipment is deadweight on household budgets.

The energy system's security shadow extends further: spending on petroleum and natural gas siphoned an estimated $30 million out of the economies of the Northwest states *each day* in 2004—nearly 3 percent of the region's economic output. And energy price spikes, which are increasingly common, are among the leading triggers of inflation and recession. The California electricity crisis of 2001, for example, deepened Cascadia's recession by sucking as much as $6 billion out of the region.

Energy's environmental shadow is better known. The power infrastructure has decimated wild salmon runs by blocking the region's rivers with dams, as shown in the maps of dam locations on pages 44 and 45. Fossil-fuel combustion is responsible for most of the region's emissions of local air pollutants and of climate-changing greenhouse gases—a global security issue that rivals even terrorism—and tankers pose the gravest water-pollution risk: massive oil spills.

CLEAN ENERGY

The key to defusing these threats is the more decentralized, resilient, and self-reliant energy infrastructure made possible through rapid gains in efficiency. Yet in 2004, despite elevated prices, energy efficiency actually suffered; the Pacific Northwest's performance on the Cascadia Scorecard's energy indicator deteriorated an estimated 1.5 percent—the equivalent of 11 extra gallons of gasoline per person per year (see Figure 10). The energy indicator did, however, remain about 3 percent below its all-time, 1999 high. (This indicator uses per capita consumption of highway fuels and nonindustrial electricity as a proxy for total energy use, as discussed in *Cascadia Scorecard 2004*. Highway fuels and non-industrial electricity usually move in tandem with total energy use and are reported much more quickly and reliably.)

From a longer view, energy use is stuck in the same range it has occupied for 25 years (see Figure 11), a range that makes energy the region's weakest-performing Scorecard indicator. Some areas of Cascadia do worse than others. Residents of the Northwest states, for example, use 45 percent more highway fuel and nonindustrial electricity apiece than BC residents. But the fundamental story of the past quarter century is this: rapidly rising technological efficiency has barely kept pace with expanding appetites.

Fortunately, new technologies, business models, and policy approaches offer to unstick the energy system, unleashing rapid gains that can wring dramatically more service from each unit of energy and turn the region toward secure, decentralized supplies. This clean-energy revolution involves the application of digital technology, advanced materials, and other new tools to energy generation and to transportation, buildings, and industry. And scores of Cascadian companies are already leading the way, generating sales measured in the billions of dollars.

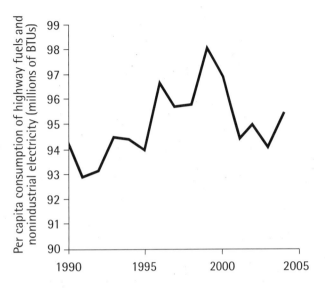

Figure 10. Cascadians used more fuel and power in 2004, despite high prices.

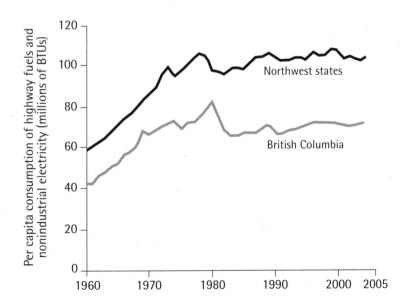

Figure 11. Residents of the Northwest states use 45 percent more energy apiece than British Columbians.

Like other innovations that bring security through design, clean energy creates compounding, mutually reinforcing benefits

These approaches deal head-on with the largest energy security problem: the architecture of the system itself. Cascadia's energy infrastructure is inherently unsafe because of its reliance on a few, centralized facilities: seven refineries, five oil pipelines, five natural gas pipelines, and roughly two dozen major transmission lines. Systems that are secure by design are versatile, resilient, redundant, and decentralized: they rely on thousands of dispersed, interconnected agents, each flexible and responsive.

"Hardening" the existing infrastructure by, for example, reinforcing pipelines and patrolling transmission towers is the reflexive security strategy, and some hardening is justified. Diversifying the existing infrastructure, through construction of a thicker web of pipe- and power lines, would help, too. But both approaches can make only marginal improvements, and they both raise the cost of energy, slowing the economy and taxing household budgets. Security through clean energy, on the other hand, saves money; it yields returns that can help finance further progress. Like other innovations that bring security through design, clean energy creates compounding, mutually reinforcing benefits.

The Northwest Power and Conservation Council (NPCC), the federally mandated regional coordinator of the Northwest states' electricity system, is pushing in this direction by encouraging utility investment in "demand response"—systems that allow utilities to temporarily turn off certain power-using devices on the consumers' side of the meter. Demand-response programs, such as the experimental Non-Wires Solutions project of the Bonneville Power Administration, recruit consumers (usually businesses) who agree to such cutbacks in exchange for cheaper rates. Demand response allows the Northwest to avoid the construction of expensive "peaking" power plants or the purchase of expensive peak power on the spot market. Demand response is also a security booster: if large transmission lines are attacked, demand response can keep vital functions operating. It would even help in the event of the loss of natural gas pipelines, since some 22 percent of the region's natural gas goes into power plants.

The Pacific Northwest National Laboratory in Richland, Washington, is taking demand response to a higher level of sophistication. The "smart grid" electronic tools they and others are developing will allow millions of electricity-using and -generating devices to adjust their operation to real-time grid conditions. If demand and prices soar, for example, preprogrammed "smart-grid" thermostats would ease up. If attackers were to disable a transmission line, decentralized energy sources such as co-generators in factories would feed power into the grid. The result: a smart grid would largely heal itself.

Demand response and the smart grid allow instantaneous rebalancing of power and gas demand. But they are only the tip of the efficiency iceberg: the potential to improve energy efficiency at a profit has actually grown over time. This fact may be surprising, considering that Cascadia has been investing in energy efficiency for a quarter century, with respectable success. The Northwest states' electricity diet, for example, is at least 10 percent smaller now than it would have been without the regional efficiency programs coordinated by NPCC since 1980. British Columbia has saved electricity at an even faster annual pace since 1990.

Yet new energy-saving technologies keep emerging more quickly than they can be deployed. In just the past five years, for example, compact-fluorescent lamps got small enough and versatile enough to work in almost all light sockets, and their price fell an astounding 75 percent. The application of dozens of similarly ingenious technologies—more-frugal DC converters in the region's roughly 100 million TVs, VCRs, and credit-card machines; rooftop cooling units that are smart enough to circulate air from the outdoors when the temperature is right rather than continuing to pump machine-chilled air; light-emitting-diode (LED) exit signs that use 5 percent as much power as the incandescent bulbs still installed in 80 percent of commercial buildings; and on and on—is the cheapest, most profitable, least polluting, and most pro-jobs energy strategy. It is also the most secure: the less electricity needed, the more likely that even a sabotaged grid can provide it.

The provincewide public utility BC Hydro and the NPCC both know this. BC Hydro, for example, sees enough energy efficiency opportunities to allow it 40 percent greater energy savings in the next 10 years than it achieved in the past 10. NPCC's 2004 draft of its next 20-year plan also sees future savings exceeding past savings. It identifies so much cost-effective efficiency that it calls for no new power plants, except wind farms, for at least 5 years. For the duration of the plan, efficiency would be by far the biggest, cheapest source of new energy, followed by wind power.

Neither NPCC nor BC Hydro is likely to succeed in implementing its plans unless it can decouple utility profits from electricity sales— a systemic innovation discussed in the next chapter. But fortunately, with that change there is no reason NPCC and BC Hydro cannot outperform their plans substantially. Neither agency, after all, has set terribly aggressive targets. California recently established mandatory statewide efficiency goals for utilities that are at least 50 percent more ambitious. And California's new policy will call on gas utilities to match the electricity sector in its commitment to saving energy—a long-overdue innovation.

FUELING TRANSPORTATION

If anything, the efficiency potential in transportation is larger, because vehicles are replaced more quickly than buildings. The typical car or light truck in the United States operates for just 14 years. Unfortunately, fuel economy improvements in Cascadia have been completely wiped out by rising vehicle weight, as SUVs and other light trucks have gained popularity. (The tragic irony, of course, is that SUVs, which many drivers buy for their supposed added safety, are actually less safe for people in them than are regular automobiles. And they are an even greater menace to people in other vehicles.)

In public consciousness, Cascadia's recent vehicle trends are epitomized by the Hummer, a four-wheeled emblem of security. But in the marketplace, Hummers and other jumbo SUVs are actually being

THE CASCADIA SCORECARD'S FOREST STUDY AREAS

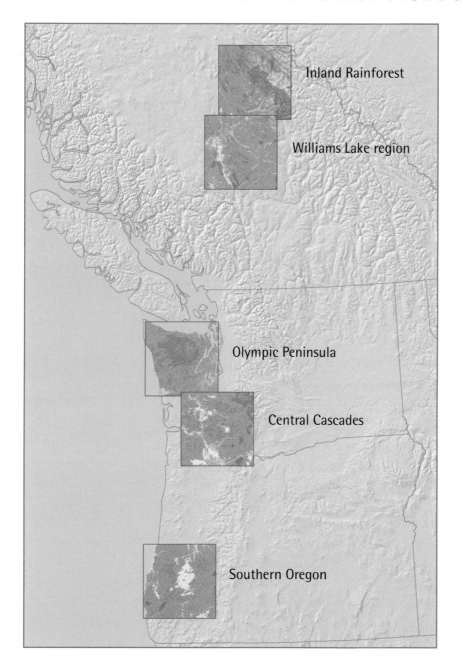

Inland Rainforest

Williams Lake region

Olympic Peninsula

Central Cascades

Southern Oregon

The five areas monitored by the Scorecard encompass about 15 percent of Cascadia's forests. Map by CommEn Space.

See all Scorecard maps and animated versions at *www.northwestwatch.org.*

LIFE EXPECTANCY IN CASCADIA

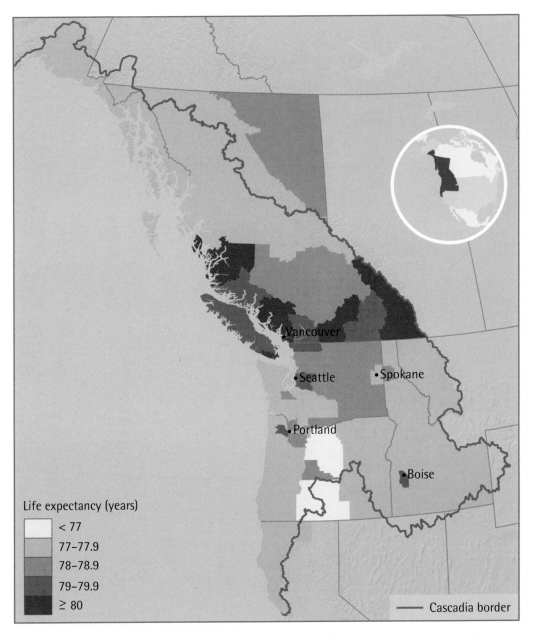

On average, residents of British Columbia live about two years longer than residents of the Northwest states. Map by CommEn Space.

AVERAGE FAMILY SIZE ACROSS THE NORTHWEST

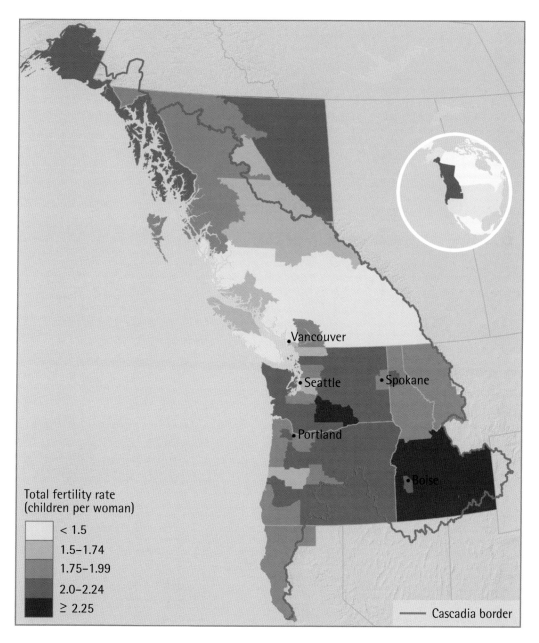

Total fertility rate
(children per woman)

- < 1.5
- 1.5–1.74
- 1.75–1.99
- 2.0–2.24
- ≥ 2.25

—— Cascadia border

Vancouver

Seattle

Spokane

Portland

Boise

Southern Idaho has Cascadia's largest average family size.
Map by CommEn Space.

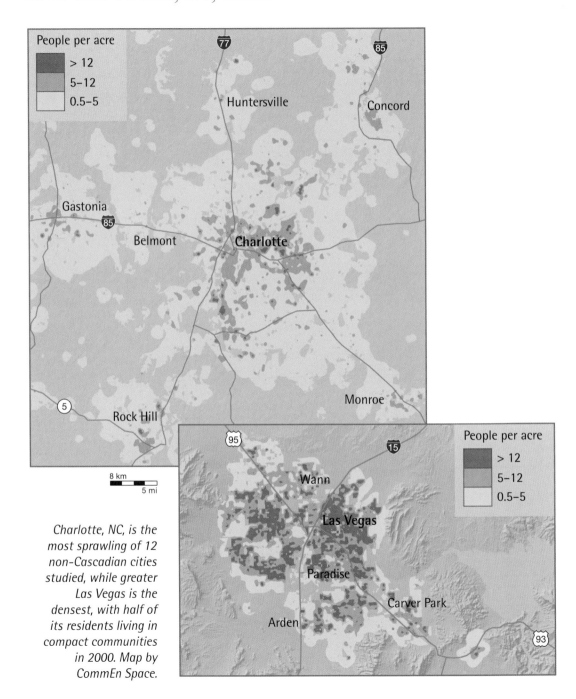

People per acre

> 12
5–12
0.5–5

Huntersville

Concord

Gastonia

Belmont

Charlotte

Monroe

Rock Hill

8 km
5 mi

People per acre

> 12
5–12
0.5–5

Wann

Las Vegas

Paradise

Carver Park

Arden

Charlotte, NC, is the most sprawling of 12 non-Cascadian cities studied, while greater Las Vegas is the densest, with half of its residents living in compact communities in 2000. Map by CommEn Space.

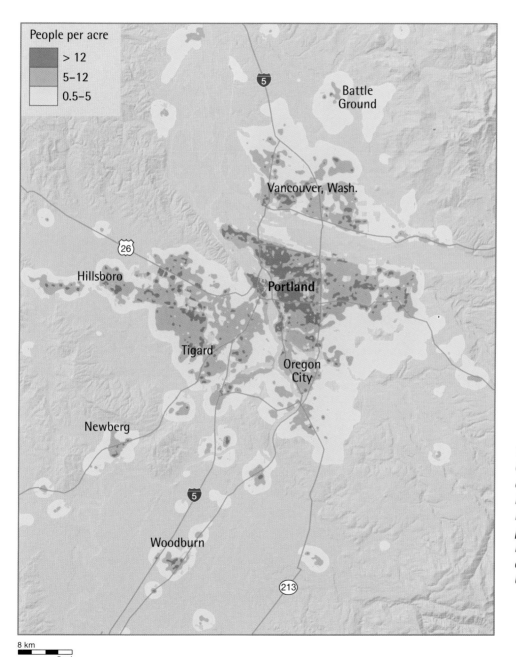

People per acre
- > 12
- 5–12
- 0.5–5

Battle Ground

Vancouver, Wash.

Hillsboro

Portland

Tigard

Oregon City

Newberg

Woodburn

8 km

5 mi

Though Portland, OR, isn't as compact as arid Las Vegas, it has excelled in recent years at protecting rural land from suburban development. Map by CommEn Space.

THE PROLIFERATION OF DAMS IN CASCADIA, 1930–98

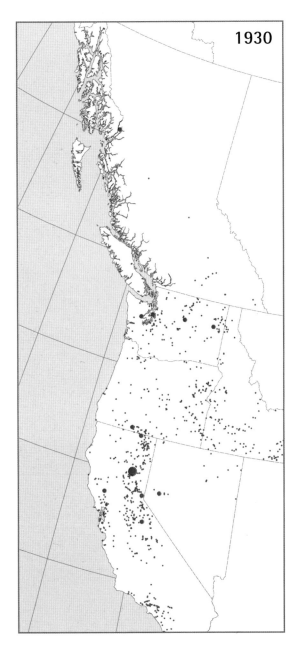

1930

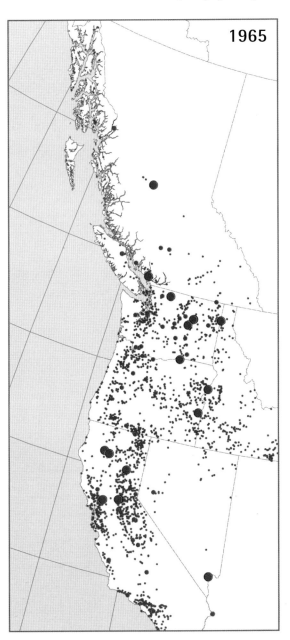

1965

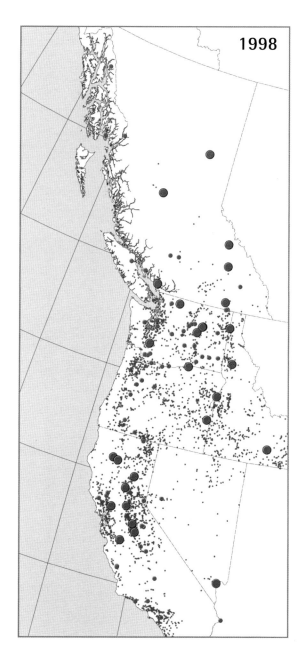

1998

Over the past 70 years, the Northwest's power infrastructure has decimated wild salmon runs by blocking the region's rivers with dams.
Maps reprinted by permission of Ecotrust.
www.ecotrust.org

Dams by water capacity
·   < 250,000 acre-feet
•   250,000–1 million acre-feet
●   > 1 million acre-feet

These maps omit dams less than 6 feet in height and with a storage capacity of less than 15 acre-feet.

100   0   300
miles

OIL PIPELINES IN CASCADIA

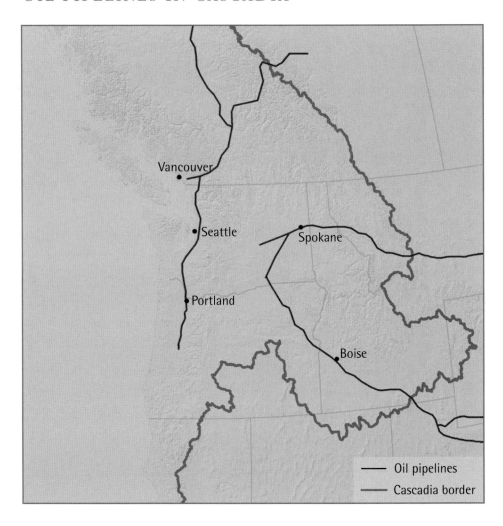

Cascadia's transportation system is reliant on a small number of oil pipelines. Map by CommEn Space.

NATURAL GAS PIPELINES IN CASCADIA

The Northwest's natural gas comes across the
Canadian Rockies through two pipelines, and
from Wyoming and other Rocky Mountain
states via a third. Map by CommEn Space.

TRANSMISSION LINES IN CASCADIA

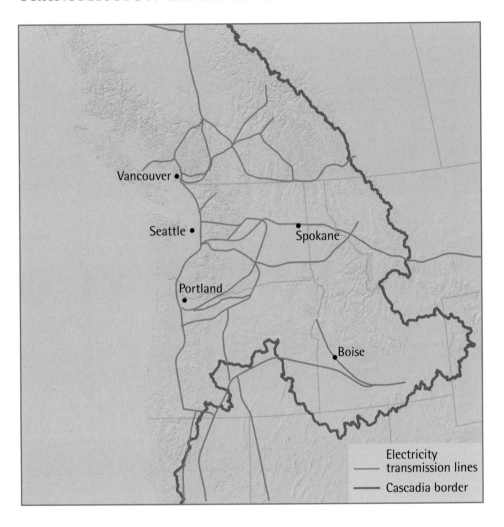

Vancouver

Seattle

Spokane

Portland

Boise

Electricity
transmission lines
Cascadia border

*The region's power network is more
secure than the oil and gas pipeline
infrastructure, but it is less stable—a
massive, interconnected balancing act.
Map by CommEn Space.*

eclipsed by something less armored but more ingenious and, in the final analysis, more secure: the hybrid-electric engine. Hybrid vehicles were introduced in 1999, seven years after Hummers, but by July 2004 had outsold them almost six to one. And while Hummer sales stagnated in 2004, hybrids rocketed out of showrooms. Cascadians who wanted the award-winning 2004 Toyota Prius, for example, typically faced waits of six months or longer.

Hybrids and Hummers are little more than the bookends of the car world; in Washington, they make up just 1 in 500 passenger vehicles. But the drama they have played out—with the unheralded victory going to the cars that travel four times as far on each unit of fuel—augurs well for Cascadia's future. A more efficient fleet sends fewer dollars out of the region and fewer pollutants into the atmosphere; it also buffers the region against pipeline disruption and oil price hikes.

The most comprehensive and authoritative recent assessment of the transportation future is the Rocky Mountain Institute's (RMI) encyclopedic 2004 volume *Winning the Oil Endgame*. In it, Amory Lovins and his research team make a compelling case that the combination of advanced hybrid engines with ultralight (but ultrasafe) vehicle designs can yield at least a doubling of fuel economy, while producing vehicles that are better in almost every way. In fact, the report's authors make a strong case for quadrupled-efficiency vehicles and even for midsize SUVs that get 99 miles per gallon. Such cars and trucks—combined with similar improvements in other oil-using sectors—could save half of Cascadia's projected 2025 petroleum consumption. And it could do so for the equivalent of $12 per barrel conserved. As Lovins and his coauthors write, the fuel in such vehicles' tanks combined with their added range "acts as a fine-grained, highly distributed Strategic Petroleum Reserve—already delivered to customers, presenting no high-value targets, invulnerable to cascading system failures (such as vulnerable pipeline networks), and profitable to boot."

Even if RMI is too optimistic, the efficiency potential for vehicles is large. A 2002 technical assessment by the National Research Council

A more efficient vehicle fleet sends fewer dollars out of the region and fewer pollutants into the atmosphere

(NRC) concluded that over 10 to 15 years, fuel economy could rise from an average of 27 miles per gallon to 41 miles per gallon, costing somewhere between $2,350 and $3,050 extra per vehicle. That cost would be worth paying even in strict financial terms; it would pay for itself about twice over in fuel savings during the vehicle's operating life. (The report's excessive pessimism became apparent within months when the 2004 Prius entered the market, triply beating NRC's projections: it got better mileage, at a lower price, a decade early.)

The best news for Cascadia concerning this impending revolution in vehicle efficiency is that it could prove a huge boon to the region's high-wage job base. Already, the North American leader in manufacturing efficient, ultralight vehicles is not in Detroit but in the Pacific Northwest. It's Boeing, whose next-generation jet (the 7E7) will be the most efficient airplane in the sky by at least 20 percent, partly thanks to the company's wholesale embrace of advanced, light-but-strong carbon-fiber polymers.

This impending revolution in vehicle efficiency could prove a huge boon to the region's high-wage job base

Boeing, the Northwest's largest manufacturing employer, is zealous about saving energy, because fuel economy is key to airline profits. The industry loses some $180 million a year for every one-penny rise in the price of a gallon of jet fuel. The 7E7 will likely reach at least 30 percent fuel savings (compared with Airbus's next jet, the A380) on many international routes by enabling point-to-point flight patterns. The Boeing jet's modest size and extended range will allow airlines to profitably connect most origins and destinations directly, rather than wasting fuel (and time) shuttling passengers through off-route "hub" airports. To compete with the 7E7, Airbus announced plans in December 2004 to begin designing a similar plane of its own.

The Northwest's second biggest vehicle maker, heavy-truck manufacturer PACCAR, has as much to gain from efficiency as Boeing. Trucking, like commercial aviation, is among the industries most exposed to fuel costs: diesel price spikes commonly precipitate waves of bankruptcies among truckers. And trucking is amenable to the same fuel-saving innovations that work for smaller vehicles: ultralight materials, better aerodynamics, and improved engines have the power to double fuel economy or more, for about 25 cents per gallon (8 Canadian cents per liter) of diesel fuel saved.

The profitable efficiency potential in transportation grows from impressive to staggering when one considers not just vehicle engineering but the architecture of transportation systems. More-compact, walkable communities, which substitute proximity for mobility, can reduce driving by as much as two-thirds and improve health too. Congestion pricing—variable, electronic tolls that eliminate traffic jams—improves vehicles' actual (as opposed to rated) fuel economy by preventing stop-and-start driving. Mileage-based auto insurance—now being market-tested in Minnesota, Australia, the Netherlands, and the United Kingdom—is inching toward implementation in the Northwest, promising savings of fuel (and money) of 10 percent or more. Transit improvements; vanpool, carpool, and car-sharing programs; pedestrian infrastructure investments; and a variety of innovations in how parking is regulated and taxed can also render internal combustion less necessary.

Together, these and other systemic innovations might lead Cascadians to eliminate as much as another quarter of their highway fuel consumption, beyond the 50 percent reduction from vehicle improvements. And Cascadia could get some—perhaps much—of the remaining quarter from plant-based "cellulose ethanol." Best estimates from Oak Ridge National Laboratory, Washington State University, and the Oregon Department of Energy are that the region could meet at least 5 percent and possibly more than 20 percent of its current gasoline demand with this locally produced fuel.

Unlike biodiesel and conventional ethanol—the large-scale production of which ultimately creates competition for food crops such as soybeans and corn—cellulose ethanol comes from crop and forest residues, urban wastes, and even grass clippings. This quick-maturing technology may prove a bonanza for the rural Northwest. The Canadian firm Iogen is hoping to build a 50-million-gallon-a-year facility in Idaho to spin wheat straw into motor fuels. This plant would likely spend

$30 million a year on straw. At that rate, rural Cascadians could reap at least $250 million a year selling residues to biorefiners—an amount almost half the value of Idaho's potato harvest. (On more optimistic assumptions, rural Cascadians could earn more than $1 billion a year from residue sales—roughly equal to Washington's apple revenue.) Royalties from wind farming, another possible bonanza for farmers and ranchers, would be additional.

Hydrogen's environmental benefits are well understood, but its security benefits are also great

The final step of the clean-energy revolution could be hydrogen and fuel cells, and again Cascadia has world-leading firms, such as Ballard Power Systems of Burnaby, British Columbia. Emissions-free and versatile, hydrogen is now regarded in many circles as the dream fuel for both transportation and distributed power generation. But most informed observers expect the hydrogen economy to be several decades in the future. Debate now centers on when and how hydrogen will emerge as a serious competitor to the stalwarts of today's energy system.

Hydrogen's environmental benefits are well understood, but its security benefits are also great: the smart grid and distributed fuel cells are made for each other. Freestanding fuel cells and even fuel cell–powered vehicles could be engineered to plug into the grid and serve as backup or peaking power sources. Highway fuels and electricity, in other words, would become interchangeable, which means redundant, which means secure. And hydrogen generation and distribution can be far more flexible and decentralized than the current fossil-fuel infrastructure.

A stronger, safer economy for Cascadia depends on shifting away from inefficient, centralized systems of distribution for fuel and power toward more-dispersed, interconnected, and resilient ones. Fortunately, this transition has long since begun. It comes in small steps, each of them profitable to investors and advantageous to communities in the short run. And each step builds momentum for the next. A little better steering from the region's governments—the topic of the next chapter—is the catalyst that could bring the clean-energy revolution to liftoff.

CONCLUSION:
SECURITY BY DESIGN

Imagine if a foreign power had seized Cascadia's communities and imposed an economy that shortened lives unnecessarily, that mired half a million children in poverty, that laid out cities in which travel was nearly impossible without a private car or truck, and that razed forests and endangered the salmon and other animals that give spirit to the place. And imagine that these outsiders upholstered northwesterners' living spaces with suspected poisons, which soon began appearing in mothers' breastmilk.

Surely, northwesterners would rise in rebellion.

That they do not is testament to the power of business as usual. Threats from the outside, even if their likelihood is remote, galvanize humans to action. But threats that emerge from the way people have set up their lives and society—the threats to long-term progress tracked in the Cascadia Scorecard—those threats are too easily ignored, discounted, or shrugged off as "just the way it is."

This blind spot, while lamentable, is also an opportunity. It means that quantum leaps in security—and therefore in long-term progress—are available to the region, if enough Cascadians act to make them happen. Those quantum leaps all create security by design. They reorient dysfunctional systems around progress that is resilient, low-risk, and stable. Such reorientations are sorely needed in a place that has so many advantages but that nonetheless lags far behind the world's leaders on one indicator after another: 58 years in sprawl, 88 years in energy, and 19 years in economy. Cascadia's slow but steady gains of the past decade have given way to stagnation in the new one; since 2001, the Scorecard average has been stuck at a 32-year gap behind best practices.

Systemic innovations that lead to security by design are plentiful. For example, if Cascadians focus consistently on making every child a wanted child, they will—simply by following the chains of cause and effect—take actions that improve access to health care and contraceptive services, that lower poverty rates among children, and that combat sexual abuse. All of these social ills markedly elevate unintended pregnancy rates. As bonuses, the region will reap improved child development; lowered rates of poverty, out-of-wedlock births, and single parenting; higher rates of marriage; and the environmental (and traffic) benefits of slower population growth.

Likewise, combating sprawl through good urban design—building neighborhoods compact enough that every eight-year-old can walk to a library—brings compounding, mutually reinforcing benefits for jobs, nature, human health, community, and security. It replaces the vicious circle of worsening traffic and air quality, rising energy costs, and a fragmenting countryside with a virtuous circle of less driving, traffic, and energy use, and more time, money, and open space.

Similarly, if the Pacific Northwest adopts an approach to synthetic compounds such as PBDEs that insists on proving safety first, before the widespread distribution of these compounds, the benefits will multiply. Contamination will decline, massive cleanup and remediation costs will disappear, and the health of both humans and wildlife will be spared future insults.

Above all, if Cascadia embraces the clean-energy revolution, it can unleash a self-propelling process of improvement and social benefit that starts with more profit and jobs and runs through to a tamper-resistant energy system. The clean-energy revolution, which could be as important to the next decade as the Internet was to the last, is already beginning. Collective action through Cascadia's governments needs only to hasten it through three steps: stepping up to "clean car" standards; hitching utilities' bottom lines to their customers' efficiency; and breaking new ground with innovative incentives called "feebates."

A powerful next step for the Northwest states would be to join together and commit to California-style vehicle emission standards for carbon dioxide. These clean-car standards, phased in from 2008 to 2016, will trim petroleum use in new vehicles by as much as 30 percent. British Columbia is already on board by virtue of Canada's national commitment to a 25 percent drop in emissions per mile by 2010, an even more ambitious target than California's. By joining with their neighbors to the north and south, the Northwest states can help to leverage change in the entire auto industry.

Cascadia could further bolster clean energy by adopting reforms that would ensure the region not only meets but exceeds the Northwest Power and Conservation Council's and BC Hydro's newest efficiency-centered plans, perhaps matching California's 50-percent-higher ambitions. During the late 1990s, the region got lazy about electrical efficiency investments, lulled by a temporary glut of cheap natural gas–fired power. In 1999, the Northwest states accomplished scarcely one-third of the efficiency gains stipulated in the not-so-ambitious NPCC plan then in effect. The region's natural gas utilities have never pursued efficiency with as much conviction as warranted. More-concerted encouragement of efficiency, and the addition of more renewables, could not only meet all demand but also begin to supplant existing fossil fuel–fired power plants, according to 2003 research by the independent Tellus Institute in Boston.

Along with conventional approaches to this goal such as revising building codes, Cascadia could put wind in the sails of efficiency by making it more profitable for utilities. Utilities are not like other companies. Their profits are dictated by state utility regulators, based on complicated formulas. At present, profits rise in direct proportion to sales, so utility investments in improving efficiency can drain away profits. In the case of PacifiCorp, a Portland-based investor-owned utility that serves parts of the Northwest states, every investment that allows its 121,000 Washington state customers to save 1 percent of their power

A powerful next step for the Northwest states would be to join together and commit to California-style vehicle emission standards

through better efficiency subtracts well over $1 million from shareholders' earnings in the first year. Such a move subtracts an equal amount in each subsequent year, often for a decade or more. Not surprisingly, many utilities are halfhearted about efficiency, even if they are legally obligated to encourage it.

Decoupling helped convert Puget Sound Power and Light from a laggard to a leader in energy efficiency

But by decoupling sales from earnings, utility regulators can write Cascadia's long-term progress and security into utilities' bottom lines and turn utilities—precisely the organizations that have the requisite know-how and capital—into vanguards of the clean-energy revolution. At present, only one US Cascadian utility has decoupled rates: NW Natural, a Portland-based gas company. An assessment in 2005 will tabulate the benefits, but earlier experience is encouraging. For example, Puget Sound Power and Light (now Puget Sound Energy) operated under a decoupling rule from 1991 to 1996 before a tangentially related lawsuit—and more importantly, the ill-fated electric deregulation movement—put decoupling on hold.

Decoupling helped convert Puget Sound Power and Light from a laggard to a leader in energy efficiency. In its first decoupled year, the company's efficiency programs saved almost as much electricity as they had saved during the three previous years combined. In its second year, it boosted savings another 60 percent and single-handedly accounted for 40 percent of all electricity savings in the Northwest states—outdoing even the regionwide federal Bonneville Power Administration—at half the cost. Decoupling is returning to the fore of regional policy debates, just in time to turbocharge implementation of NPCC and BC Hydro's efficiency-centered plans.

A systemic innovation with potential to greatly accelerate the spread of clean-car technology, and other energy-efficient devices, is the adoption of feebates. These point-of-purchase incentives—graduated fees charged to the buyers of less-efficient products that fund graduated rebates given to the buyers of more-efficient ones—systematically nudge manufacturers and consumers toward saving energy. The more efficient the car or other energy-using device, the smaller the fee—or bigger the rebate. Feebates, unlike CAFE standards and building codes, keep efficiency snowballing: the feebates reset themselves each year at the average energy efficiency of new models.

Feebates correct documented market failures, such as the "payback gap" between energy consumers and producers. Motorists refuse to pay for fuel-economy improvements that take more than three years to pay for themselves in fuel savings, while oil companies typically drill in remote locations hoping to recoup their costs and begin earning profits much further down the road. Indeed, they operate in a business where payback periods as short as three years are rare exceptions. The result is a massive, economy-wide misallocation of resources that results in lost jobs, amplified environmental harm, and higher costs for consumers. Feebates fix this market flaw by making purchase prices a better reflection of life-cycle costs—by making prices tell the truth.

Cascadia has come close to feebates twice before, in California in 1990 and in British Columbia in 2000. In both cases, political conditions were not quite right. The Canadian federal government is now considering feebates as part of its climate action plan. And the West Coast Governors' Global Warming Initiative, a regional effort to combat climate change, presents the perfect political opportunity to introduce synchronized regionwide feebates on new vehicles, appliances, and other energy-using devices.

With clean-car standards, profit-motivated utilities investing in their customers' efficiency, and revenue-neutral feebates, clean energy will surge. And the insecurity of Cascadia's current energy system will give way to an array of benefits: a rekindled farm economy; strengthened, high-wage aerospace and truck-making sectors; an emerging industrial cluster in advanced materials, green buildings, energy efficiency and renewables, fuel-cell energy, and tools for the smart grid; the continuous economic stimulus of keeping up to $10 billion a year circulating locally rather than leaking away from the region; plummeting emissions of pollution to the air; world leadership on slowing climate change; and an energy system that is largely immune to "people of mass destruction."

For energy—as for population, sprawl, pollution, and the other Cascadia Scorecard trends—security, like progress, lies in design. It lies in converting perverse and dysfunctional systems into resilient, self-correcting ones. It lies in emulating the alchemy of the Pacific Northwest's natural ecosystems, which takes sunshine and muck and transforms them into whale song, the fight of steelhead on the line, and other means of sustenance and inspiration. Best of all, the rewards of success in this endeavor are as immediate and tangible for present northwesterners as they are essential for the next generation of northwesterners: Cascadia becomes a model of *se cura*, of being free (or, at least, freer) from care.

ACKNOWLEDGMENTS

If we measured regional progress toward sustainability by the number of talented and hardworking Cascadians who help Northwest Environment Watch, then 2004's results show that we are well on our way.

We'll start with the creators of *Cascadia Scorecard 2005*. It was written by Alan Thein Durning and Clark Williams-Derry, with research assistance from John Abbotts and Matt Schoellhamer. Others who helped with research include Eric de Place, Jocelyn Hittle, and Todd Burley; and CommEn Space staff Josh Livni, Tim Schaub, Chris Davis, and Hiroo Imaki, who created most of the maps presented in the book and online. We also thank designer Jennifer Shontz, editor Julie Van Pelt, and proofreader Sherri Schultz; and, for their helpful comments, reviewers Ralph Cavanagh, Mark Jaccard, and Patrick Mazza.

We are grateful to our many volunteers for their valuable contributions in 2004, including communications interns Todd Burley (also a research intern), Elizabeth Burton, and Michèle Savelle; research interns Matt Schoellhamer and Jocelyn Hittle; and the many office volunteers, volunteer consultants, and others who donated time and skills, including Page Atcheson, Yoram Bauman, Tom DeCory-Keen, Amy Durning, Gary Durning, Kathryn Durning, Peter Durning, Benjamin Facer, Theresa Fenton, Carrie Fox, KC Golden, Michael Greenberg, Ryan Hawkes, Ellen Joan Hutchinson, Bill Kint, Mark Kotzer, Robert Lowry, Lyn McCollum, Ethan Meginnes, Ashley Mitchell, Tanya Niemeyer, Carol Olson, Mary Peterson, Dov Sherman, and Melissa Shaw. And as he heads east in 2005, we'd particularly like to thank longtime office volunteer Neal Parry for his hard work and good humor, and for carrying all those books upstairs. (We are, of course, also very grateful to our financial and in-kind supporters, whom we acknowledge in the next section.)

We would also like to thank all who contributed to our PBDE pollution study, including Linda Birnbaum, Aimee Boulanger, Delores Broten,

Mike Brown, Marcia David, Kate Davies, Tracy Deisher, Fe De Leon, Todd deVries, Jennifer Frankel-Reed, Dori Gilels, Arthur Holden, Kim Hooper, Aubrey Lau, Sonya Lunder, Tom McDonald, Elise Miller, Han Nguyen, MaryAnn O'Hara, Linda Park, Amelia Psmythe, Kim Radtke, Mark Rogge, Arnold Schecter, Erika Schreder, Margaret Sharp, Renee Sharp, Jianwen She, Manon Tanner, Michael Templin, Laurie Valeriano, Laura Weiss, and the 40 mothers who participated. We also thank other partners and experts for peer-reviewing NEW's work and assisting with outreach throughout the year.

In 2004, NEW benefited from the generosity of those who hosted, organized, or headlined events or discussion groups on our behalf: John Atcheson, Brian & Sharon Beinlich, Jeff Hallberg, Laura Retzler & Henry Wigglesworth, and Aron Thompson.

We thank the members of the NEW Advocates Society—volunteers who help us raise major gifts—for helping NEW become more sustainable: Gail Achterman, John Atcheson, Jeffrey Belt, Bill Feinberg, Jeff Hallberg, Langdon Marsh, Ethan Meginnes, Rick Meyer, Laura Retzler, Lura Smith, Aron Thompson, and David Yaden.

NEW is grateful to its board of directors for their donation of much time and support: David Yaden, chair, and Gail Achterman, John Atcheson, Alan Durning, Jeff Hallberg, Cheeying Ho, Catherine Mater, Nancy Olewiler, Gordon Price, Laura Retzler, and Aron Thompson. We also thank Aaron Contorer, who was our longest-serving board member when he left the board this year.

Finally, NEW is grateful to its hardworking staff: Alan Thein Durning, executive director; Christine Hanna, managing director; Dana Brown, bookkeeper and operations manager; Parke G. Burgess, director of donor relations; Eric de Place, senior research associate; Elisa Murray, communications director; Stacey Panek, senior development associate; Robin Simons, grants associate; Leigh Sims, senior communications associate; and Clark Williams-Derry, research director. We also thank John Abbotts, who worked as a research consultant during the latter half of 2004; and Dan Yuly, our former accountant.

OUR SUPPORTERS

CASCADIA STEWARDS COUNCIL FOUNDING MEMBERS

These individuals committed support to NEW at a major level over a minimum of three years in 2004, the Council's inaugural year. They're listed in descending order of the amount of their total commitment.

Contorer Foundation
Anonymous
Thomas & Sonya Campion
Linda S. Park & Denis G. Janky
Magali & Jeffrey Belt
Maggie Hooks & Justin Ferrari
Amy & Alan Thein Durning
Judy Pigott
Laura Retzler & Henry Wigglesworth
Jonathan Durning & Melanie Ronai
Loeb/Meginnes Foundation
Karen & Jeremy Mazner
Janet Vogelzang & Mark Cliggett
Christopher & Mary Troth
Jabe Blumenthal
Gun & Tom Denhart
John Russell & Mary Fellows
Tom & Jennifer Luce
Keith Kegley
Jeffrey & Nicole Hallberg
Langdon Marsh & Ellie Putnam
Sara Moorehead & Jeffrey Ratté
Aron Thompson, A.G. Edwards Seattle
    Financial Group
Janice & David Yaden
Gail Achterman
James L. Plummer
John Atcheson
Mark Groudine & Cynthia Putnam
Anirudh Sahni
Glenn S. Rodriguez & Molly E.R. Keating

Kristayani & Jerry Jones
Edward Mills & Irene Pasternack
Parke G. Burgess Jr.
Anonymous
JF & Leslie Baken
Paul & Donna Balle
Connie Battaile
Julian Battaile
Tony & Sue Beeman
Thomas Buxton & Terri Anderson
Jon Carder & Monique Baillargeon
Ann & Doug Christensen
Peter Donaldson
John & Jane Emrick
William Feinberg
Maradel Krummel Gale
Christine Hanna & Eugene Pitcher
Jeanette L. Henderson
Gretchen & Lyman Hull
Gretchen & Erik Jansen
Mark A. Kotzer
Bill Kramer & Melissa Cadwallader
Linda Moulder & Jerry White
Jean Marie Piserchia & Robert C. Ball
James & Rebecca Potter
Ingrid Rasch
Manya & Howard Shapiro
Jim & Jan Thomas
Birgitte B. Williams
Jeff Youngstrom & Becky Brooks
Gordon Price

GIFTS AND COMMITMENTS FOR 2004

Gifts and commitments listed were received from January 1, 2004, through December 31, 2004. NEW would additionally like to thank the approximately 400 individuals, organizations, and families who also made gifts to NEW in 2004.

$100,000 or more
The Russell Family Foundation

$25,000–$99,999
The Brainerd Foundation
The Bullitt Foundation
Contorer Foundation
Horizons Foundation
Social Venture Partners

$10,000–$24,999
Campaign for America's Wilderness for
    Thomas & Sonya Campion
Carolyn Foundation
Microsoft Matching Gifts Program
Linda Park & Denis Janky
Seattle Biotech Legacy Foundation
Up the River Endeavors
The Winslow Advised Fund

$1,000–$9,999
Anonymous (4)
Gail Achterman
John Atcheson
Leslie & Jeffrey Baken
Paul & Donna Balle
Connie Battaile
Julian Battaile
Jeffrey & Magali Belt
Jabe Blumenthal
Parke G. Burgess Jr.
Victoria Burwell
Thomas Buxton & Terri Anderson
Jon Carder & Monique Baillargeon

Charitable Gift Fund for Carrie & Barry Saxifrage
Ann & Doug Christensen
Mary A. Crocker Trust for Elizabeth Atcheson
Gun & Tom Denhart
Amy & Alan Thein Durning
Jonathan Durning & Melanie Ronai
John & Jane Emrick
William Feinberg
Robert & Judy Fisher
Maradel Krummel Gale
Hellmut & Marcy Golde
Nigel Green & Lisa Chin
Jeffrey & Nicole Hallberg
Christine Hanna & Eugene Pitcher
Harris Bank Foundation
Jeanette L. Henderson
George H. Hess
Maggie Hooks & Justin Ferrari
David Huffaker & Barbara Staley
Gretchen & Lyman Hull
Barbara O. Jackson
Gretchen & Erik Jansen
Harvey Jones & Nancy Iannucci
Jubitz Family Foundation
Keith Kegley
Mark A. Kotzer
Bill Kramer & Melissa Cadwallader
Loeb/Meginnes Foundation
Thomas & Jennifer Luce
Langdon Marsh & Ellie Putnam
Catherine Mater
Karen & Jeremy Mazner
Robert & Betty McInnes
Edward Mills & Irene Pasternack

Sara Moorehead & Jeffrey Ratté
Linda Moulder & Jerry White
Oregon Community Foundation for
    Kristayani & Jerry Jones
Judy Pigott
Jean Marie Piserchia & Robert C. Ball
James L. Plummer
James & Rebecca Potter
Cynthia Putnam & Mark Groudine
Ingrid Rasch
Thomas & Sally Reeve
Laura Retzler & Henry Wigglesworth
Faye & Mike Richardson
Glenn S. Rodriguez & Molly E.R. Keating
John Russell & Mary Fellows
Anirudh Sahni
John & Lorrie Schleg
Manya & Howard Shapiro
Starbucks Coffee Company
Jim & Jan Thomas
Aron Thompson, A.G. Edwards Seattle
    Financial Group
Christopher & Mary Troth
Janet Vogelzang & Mark Cliggett
Washington Mutual Matching Gift Program
Winky Foundation
Doug & Maggie Walker/WRQ
Lawrence R. Weisberg
Birgitte B. Williams
Janice & David Yaden

$250–$999

Amgen Foundation
Pauline & Lloyd Anderson
Gordon Battaile
Jonathan & Erin Becker
Tony & Sue Beeman

Mary Anne Christy & Mark Klebanoff
Curtis DeGasperi & Sara Waterman
Jean & Marvin Durning
Erik W. Fisher
Albert E. Foster
Diana Gale & Jerry Hillis
Wendy Green
Jere & Raymond Grimm
William & Barbara Harris
Sara S. Hinckley
Vincent Houmes
The Arie Kurtzig Memorial Fund
Jean Walden Kershner
Frances & David Korten
Nancy-Clair Laird & Steven McInaney
Matt & Leslie Leber
John A. Lee
Linda Magee & Craig Fisk
John & Hanna Liv Mahlum Trust
David Marshak
Richard Meyer & Aleta Howard
Leonard E. Pavelka
The Pfizer Foundation Matching Gifts Program
Gordon Price
Allen & Laura Puckett
Katherine A. Randolph & Kyle Wang
Carol D. Roberts
Scott & C. Joan Sandberg
Peter & Rita Thein
Kristopher & Jo Ann Townsend
Daniell Walters
Kathryn E. Wilbur
Karen & George Bray
David Callahan & Rose Bolson
Jeffrey Youngstrom & Rebecca Brooks
Kenneth & Yvonne Zick

IN-KIND DONATIONS

We are grateful to the following individuals and organizations who donated valuable services or material gifts to NEW in 2004.

John Atcheson
Brian & Sharon Beinlich
Steven Cristol, Cristol & Associates
Gordon Dow
Erik & Gretchen Jansen
Jubitz Family Foundation
Ashley Mitchell
Nancy Olewiler

Laura Puckett, DLA Piper Rudnick Gray Cary
Laura Retzler & Henry Wigglesworth
Lura Smith & Bill Schubach
Social Venture Partners
Glenn Thomas, Producing Future
Aron Thompson, A.G. Edwards Seattle
    Financial Group
Steve Trautman